Colors

red

orange

yellow

green

blue

purple

pink

white

black

brown

What color is the apple?

The apple is red.

What color is the banana?

The banana is yellow.

What color are the shoes?

The shoes are black.

What color are the sandals?

The sandals are pink.

What color is the cup?

The cup is red.

What color is the bowl?

The bowl is green.

What color are the carrots?

The carrots are orange.

What color are the grapes?

The grapes are purple.

What color is the jacket?

The jacket is blue.

What color is the scarf?

The scarf is red.

What color is the pencil?

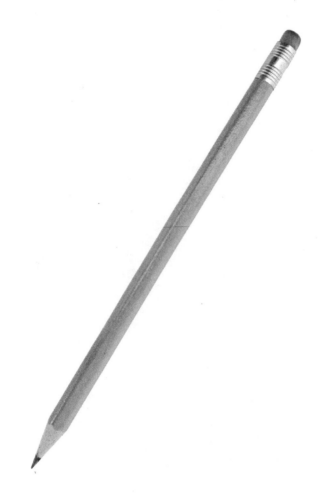

The pencil is yellow.

What color is the eraser?

The eraser is pink.

What color are the tomatoes?

The tomatoes are red.

What color is the broccoli?

The broccoli is green.

What color is the bus?

The bus is yellow.

What color is the car?

The car is white.

What color is the hat?

The hat is red.

What color is the umbrella?

The umbrella is black.

What color is the sofa?

The sofa is green.

What color is the table?

The table is brown.

Easy English Readers:
Colors

www.teachabcenglish.com

2017

Made in the USA
San Bernardino, CA
12 March 2019